Sustenance

Feed the Body: Nourish the Soul

A collection of plant based, gluten free recipes
created for:

Vida Asana School of Yoga in Costa Rica

By Heather Hands

Photos by Elaina Cochran & Heather Hands

Hello, thank you for inviting me into your kitchen! My intention with this book is to make available to alumni and the community at large, the recipes that I created for Vida Asana School of Yoga. Located in Playa Hermosa, Costa Rica, Vida Asana is both yoga school and eco-retreat center and boasts a mainly plant based, gluten free menu for guests. In general the recipes are all simple to follow on their own, but I created an easy to follow '3 Week Guide' that makes it even easier to plan meals by having on hand many pre-prepped sauces, dressings, and other components of each meal.

As you will see, there are not exactly the number of recipes needed to fill every meal within the 3 weeks, but the goal is to also spark and inspire your own creativity by filling in gaps with your personal favorites that will utilize your well stocked pantry and fresh vegetable cache. Also, as I explain a little later, the recipes are geared to bulk cooking, so there should be plenty of leftovers to eliminate a need to prepare every single meal.

You will find that the book is categorized by flavor profile, sweet, light hearty, rather than specific meal, breakfast, lunch dinner, or specific item, sucah as soup, salad, etc. This was done in an effort to organize pre-preparations which are also broken down in this way, but to appeal to the senses and cravings from a more visceral place, as opposed to the logical cerebral function.

In later pages, I explain a bit more how best to use this book, but first, I will share a small glimpse into my thoughts about food. For me, food is a lens to view society, culture, community, health, and nature. It is a focal point, the central unifying piece of humanity, an important piece in our continued evolution, and how we can find common ground to connect deeper to nature and each other.

A small glimpse into my path...

For as long as I can remember, food has been an integral part of my life. Yes, I know, we all have to eat to survive, therefore it is an integral piece to all existence. But I refer to the not so obvious survival aspect, or the 'have to', but that of how my soul has been fed. My Italian grandma's kitchen holds warm memories. My curiosity in the power of delicious food was piqued by my single father's successful attempts to woo his dates with multi-course gourmet meals, meals that he adapted from a few of his hundred or so cookbooks. Living with a Malaysian nanny to care for me while my dad traveled for his job brought yet another layer of what food meant for me from a completely different cultural perspective. We have to eat to survive, but food is so much more than mere survival.

Food is the center point of human existence. It is interwoven in our emotions, culture, desires, health, technology - our entire being. Its cultivation some 10,000 plus years ago completely changed the trajectory of society. Agriculture pushed us from hunters and gatherers to a more sedentary and stratified society. With food production relegated to the peasant classes, the ruling classes were left to grow in power and in land that was won on the backs of the peasant farmers. What a juxtaposition to where we are today. Perfectly plated and artistically driven food pictures on social media are painstakingly styled to get the perfect shot - but at what cost? Food as medicine hashtags give us hope that we can tap into the healing power of food by doing the right thing - whatever that is this week. White girl burrito shops shutting down before they began due to attacks on them for cultural appropriation. Where is the line between adaptation, appreciation, and appropriation? Superfoods trends that drive the market and the ego at the expense of the environment, and all still on the backs of distant "peasant" farmers. This is not judgment nor finger pointing, observations rather. I am complicit. We all are.

I understand the heaviness of some of these statements. That's not what this book is about, but I would be remiss to not include the 'food for thought' in how we make our choices. Certainly I am not saying to never eat chocolate again. I will be having some tonight! Rather, balance is what I desire. Being mindful of our consumption and its costs beyond the financial, and slowing down to eat with intention are keys. And most importantly, to come together in the celebration of what the earth provides us. Food is a vehicle to community, to connection to family and friends. Find joy in simple pleasures like growing or wild harvesting salad and sharing it with your community. Tap into the sustainable resources in your own community and the local superfoods that are right under our noses and likely in your own backyard!

Making coconut oil...

To try to explain the respect I have for the woman in the following photos, would necessitate peering into the most intimate places of my soul. I was fortunate enough to spend much time with her and her beautiful family, learning many traditional ways and growing a profound love for her, the culture, the land she farmed, and the sheer simplicity of this life. Do not mistake simplicity for easy, however, to live disconnected from technology (and electricity) and connected to the land requires an intense amount of physical labor, but the reward is a peaceful existence, one to which I long to return... In this photo and the following photos, you will see the process to make coconut oil by hand. The process is gathering 50-75 coconuts, husking them, cracking them, and grating each half. Each batch is then washed three times by rinsing and squeezing the pulp and retaining the wash liquid. The mixture is then covered and rests overnight, slightly fermenting from the heat of the jungle. The next morning the oil rises and is skimmed from the top. A fire is built and the oil is placed in a pot over the fire to gently simmer and remove any remaining moisture. It is then bottled and used or offered up for sale. Now reread the process above, then recall the following images and this story each time you walk down the grocery store aisles, silently thanking those who hold the traditional ways and knowledge.

3
AGROTUBERCULOS

A few notes on culture...

So many neccessary conversations are happening these days on cultural appropriation. Cultural appropriation is colonialism renamed, where the subjugator in the dominant culture uses the marketplace machine to exploit or profit from sacred traditions. It is damaging and insulting - traditional foods, ceremonial regalia, art, land, and sacred practicesthe, are flat out stolen. Indigenous and traditional cultures historically have been intentionally relegated to less desirable lands and then undermined to weaken their voice and in turn, their financial security to keep them in obscurity. Corporations are protected through intellectual property rights, but the indigenous cultures have had little to no protection and many are left impoverished through back handed "help", while some up and coming designer and their stolen "original design" are raking it in hand over fist. And now, understandably, through many efforts and aided by the unifying aspects of technology, many cultures are empowering themselves and reclaiming their birthright. Which leads to the often nebulous area of where the line exists between adaptation, appreciation, and appropriation. With tensions high and triggers worn, any hint at cultural appropriation results in a cascade of angry reactions, some of which are from an equally misinformed place as the accused. And this line can differ from person to person within the same culture even. So where is the line, and whose role is it to determine the boundary? How can evolutionary, pre-colonial, cultural history help to inform and educate us?

When you think of pasta sauce and noodles and tomato sauce, what is the first culture that comes to mind? I would assume that you are thinking about Italy right now. But as you very well may know, noodles were brought to Italy from China, and tomatoes were brought back from the Americas. The Italians didn't serve Chinese food and call it their own, they found something useful and adapted it to their culture. This example is, of course, an incredibly simplified scenario and we won't go in to the deeper history of it all, but it does demonstrate the concept of adaptation over appropriation.

But lets look back a bit further. Through an anthropological lens, it is an accepted understanding that cultures in isolation die. Marriage was a form of spreading genes to distant clans and tribes to ensure genetic diversity as well as physical survival in cases of limited resources. Intercultural trade and idea sharing was also a means of survival. Cultures shared information and traded with each other and then adapted it to meet their collective needs, engendering technological evolution, among other advances.

That is also not to say that stronger, more weaponized, pre-colonial cultures, did not conquer and subsume others, but it is a very complex subject, so for this discussion, I am over simplifying to give basic information. So yes, back to my point, cultural sharing has been integral in cultural preservation and simultaneously in its evolution. The only constant is change, therefore to place anything in a box to preserve it, only inhibits its dynamic growth, and ultimately is a death sentance. The idea is to preserve the traditional ways while allowing for evolutionary change. Easier said than done, I know. Which leads me back to cultural appreciation and adaptation, versus appropriation.

Adaptiing relevant cultural information to another culture, for the betterment of the whole, think shared farming practices or architectural design elements that help to relieve the earth's burden, is a natural part of knowledge dissemenation and shows adaptation. Taking elements of culture, especially that of the sacred, and blatantly exploiting it, think hipster in a sacred Native American headdress at a music festival, or an indigenous design that gets subtley changed and shows up on the runway of a non-indigenous designer, that is appropriating. Yet an indigenous fashion design or piece of visual art made by an indigenous designer or artist, and worn or displayed by someone from another culture, is a form of appreciation.

As far as where the line resides between each concept, that is much more difficult to determine. Understanding historical concepts of cultural evolution and that the adaptation of shared information between cultures has been happening since the beginning of time, is not a common understanding. Additionally, millenia of domination, appropriation, profiteering and silencing- passed on through transgenerational trauma and epigenetic memory, has put many historically marginalized cultures on high alert - with good reason. If you are a part of the dominant culture and are told you are appropriating, do not diminish it, honor their truth by humbly listening. Take the time to process the information and resist knee jerk reactions to minimize your discomfort. Come to the table (literally if you can) with an open heart and mind and ask to join - not dominate - the conversation.

I draw inspiration from many cultures in the food that I create, and in my travels, have shared my knowledge as well. The intent behind the action, is the most important, however, it is up to the individual to educate themselves and listen with open hearts to those whom have historically been silenced.

I ♥ NY

A few notes on food as medicine...

Food as medicine is the latest catch phrase. But what does it mean?

The common understanding of food as medicine is generally in a very western, scientific way. It provides nutrients, enzymes, minerals, antioxidants, phytonutrients, etc... in the physical form that are known to help with this ailment or that disease.

The truth is all whole plant based food is medicine. Heavily processed, chemically treated, and structurally changed pre-packaged items from the grocery store are not food. Yes it is edible, and calling it food is not only collectively accepted, but in the 50s, eating in this way was considered superior - better living through chemistry. What are labeled as superfoods are also no more medicinal than non superfoods - perhaps they have a broader nutrient profile, but the medicine of food is more than the sum of its nutrients. Every hand that touches your food from seed to table is part of that medicine. The people that guard this knowledge everyday, not as novelty, but as a way of life, they are medicine and the food they produce is medicine. Your belief structure around it will make a larger impact on your health, than the food itself.

The hearth is medicine - where you share your meals in family and community. I'm sure you have noticed that when at a party, so many people congregate in the kitchen - even if they are not eating? It is the warmth, the sheer sustenance of the hearth energy that draws people to it.

You are medicine. When we disconnect from our societally sanctioned belief structure and connect to nature at her deepest core, something magical happens. We start to understand that we are not separate from nature. We are nature. The idea of this separation came from the modern industrial world and the need to conquer wild-nature out of fear. We began to lose the ability to communicate from our heart space - the communication portal with nature, and learned to rely only on what information our brain could discern from our five senses. No wonder we became scared of nature. Our power to discern is amazing and science has my deepest respect, but we are more than our head brains, science is finally coming to this conclusion, and many other conclusions that indigenous and traditional societies have long known. And now science has isolated and mapped the hormones and pathways in which our heart perceives information and has even gone as far to say that we have brains in each of our organs, most notably in our hearts and through the enteric nervous systems in our gut, that send information to our brain to discern through our logical, empirical understandings and experiences. For a deeper understanding of this concept, see Harrod Buhner's "The Secret Teachings of Plants".

Slow down, if only for one minute each day, and try to connect to your food, to the hands that touched it along the way, to all of nature. This type of gratitude can work miracles in your life with your health.

The Recipes

First: Understand that this is not a cookbook in the traditional sense (though it can function in that way), rather, more of a manual. The recipes are geared to large batch cooking for several reasons - for prepping ease, ecological efficiency, community building, family time, and cost efficiency.

The purpose of these recipes is that they utilize the same basic ingredients reworked into a variety of flavor profiles, accented by sauces and dressings, or set off by cooking method. Many of the recipes can be folded in to the next meal, making it easy and cost effective to prepare them.

There are two ways to use this book:
1. As a guide to completely transition to a plant based diet, by offering a 3 week transition guide complete with meal planning, and pre-prepping sides and condiments that are easily stored or frozen to ease meal preparations later.
2. Or as a traditional recipe book to add more plant based options into your existing diet.

Second: Stock your pantry. You don't have to do it all at once, but you can if you want to jump in feet first. On the following pages you will find a list of dry ingredients to keep on hand. Please note that pantry items can differ based on brand, process, type, etc... So read the section regarding pantry notes to see how to make substitutions in this book.

Third: Plan for some prep time. Go through the book and read the recipes first, then make a plan for the week, or use the 3 week guide provided. In general the sauces and and dressings can be made ahead in larger quantities to store in the fridge and use at will. Get your friends or kids involved to prep together, or use the time alone as a meditation.

Fourth: Stay heart focused and keep your mind open. What energy do you want to imbue into your food?

Shopping Lists: Building your Pantry

It is important to know that you don't have to run out and buy everything on the pantry list. You can, but there are ways to organize your expenditures over the month to spread out the spending and ease the financial impact. All items that you will need for all recipes in this book are found on the next two pages. You will also find on following pages some notes about certain ingredients, and the '3 Week Guide'.

Taking some time in advance to plan your meals for the week will make an amazing difference when its time to fix dinner. These prep-ahead pantry items for longer storage on the pantry shelf, in the refrigerator, or in the freezer, will allow you to prep and store now for cooking ease later. If cooking in bulk does not suit you, most of the recipes can easily be halved to make smaller servings.

Also, if you are following the bulk prep guideline and the item is for freezing, be sure to freeze in portion sizes to suit your needs to eliminate thawing more than will be consumed in a few days.

Keep in mind that if you are not kitchen savvy, some things may seem a bit cumbersome at first, and the recipes may take longer than the times indicated. But fluidity will come with practice and these recipes can become habit and easily prepared and adjusted with ease.

Fresh Produce

Veggies/Mushrooms:

Zucchini
Carrots
Roma Tomatoes
Cherry Tomatoes
Cucumbers
Red Bell Pepper
Red Onions
Yellow Onions
Garlic
Portabella Mushrooms
or Crimini Mushrooms
Green Cabbage
Red Cabbage
Eggplant
Green Beans
Cauliflower
Broccoli
Beets
Yuka
White Sweet Potatoes
Gold Potatoes
Celery
Corn
Ginger Root
Turmeric Root

Fruit:

Mango
Pineapple
Bananas
Apples
Limes/Lemons
(use interchangeably)
Oranges
Plantains

Lettuce/Greens:

Butter/Bibb
Kale (or favorite
braising green)
Chard
Spinach

Fresh Herbs:

Basil
Tarragon
Cilantro
Parsley
Mint

A few notes on produce...

One of my passions is growing food through permaculture and organic gardening. But not everyone has this option and even with this option, there are still those things that we must source. My purpose with this book was not to force a vegan dogma, nor shame anyone for less than exceptional environmental practices. Those approaches are divisive and ultimately not effective. We are all on a path and encounter times of abundance and smooth sailing and times that are challenging where we are tired and have to shore up our spending. My goal here is to provide ways that we can help protect the Earth's resources while not killing our own selves to do so. We can make small changes that together can have a great impact. Do your best in each moment, and know that your best is a reflection of your situation in that moment. Small gestures, repeated, become habits and once they are habits, we do them with ease. Maybe today you can remember to say "no straw" to the bartender while you are drowning your sorrows. Ha! But really, small steps, incorporating more plants in your diet, less factory farmed meats, buying local when you can, knowing your farmers, and understanding the plight of farmers in other countries who grew the food not native to your area, are steps in the right direction. Cultivate gratitude each day, build a relationship with nature, go to her for healing. Once you feel the benefits of all the Earth does for us, you will want to care for her in the way one cares for a precious loved one.

These recipes were created in Costa Rica, based on what was easily available. The majority of them utilize produce that is readily grown in temperate climates as well. As I mentioned above, buying local is a beneficial community practice. But we don't all live in tropical zones, and sometimes we want a pineapple or banana...

The banana and pineapple plantations have been and are still notorious for worker and land exploitation and endangerment (poor conditions, pesticide exposure, among others). Buying organic alone does not always put you on the right side as many large tropical fruit corporations have organic sectors, with the same human rights violations. But there are ethical ways to procure these universally loved fruits.

If you live in the states, look for bananas and pineapples from Earth University located in Costa Rica, or fruits that have the fair trade sticker, indicating that the growers receive fair compensation. These may have been sourced from Ecuador, Peru, Jamaica, and other tropical nations. If those are difficult to find or you live in another country, a quick internet search and a little bit of research can help lead you to a better option.

Stocking The Pantry

Oils:

Virgin/Raw Coconut Oil
Avocado or Grapeseed Oil
Sesame Oil
Extra Virgin Olive Oil

Seeds/Nuts/Grains/Beans:

Dried Unsweetened Coconut
Sunflower Seeds
Raw Almonds
Sliced Almonds (optional)
Raw Peanuts
Raw Cashews
Chia Seeds
Black Sesame Seeds
Quinoa
Dried Black or Red Beans
Dried Garbanzo Beans
Dried Lentils

Grains/Rice/Pastas:

Oats
Brown Rice
Sushi Rice
Pad Thai Rice Noodles
Spring Roll Wrappers

Dried Fruits:

Sun Dried Tomatoes
Medjool or Deglet Dates
Cranberries/Raisins/Cherries

Various Dry Goods:

Himalayan Salt or Sea Salt
Tahini
Miso Paste
Dijon or Whole Grain Mustard
Balsamic Vinegar
Apple Cider Vinegar
Tamari or Liquid Aminos
Maple Syrup or Agave
Sugar - Raw/Coconut/Palm
Cacao Powder (cocoa powder)
Tamarind Paste

Dried Spices:

Cumin
Chili Powder
Cinnamon
Turmeric (if fresh is not available)
Italian Seasoning Blend
Oregano
Cayenne
Curry Powder

Special Equipment:

Blender
Food Processor
Nut Milk Bag
Glass Jars

Helpful But Not Necessary:

Rice Cooker
Spiralizer

A few notes on the Pantry items...

Oils: This topic alone is enough to incite panic in many as everyone seems to have an opinion. Well here is mine. Fats and oils are necessary in our diets, but not in excess. They should be healthy fats and when it comes to cooking oil, be able to handle high heat without denaturing (disrupting its molecular structure). Avocado, grapeseed, sesame and coconut oils are excellent for this purpose. I reserve extra virgin olive oil for salad dressings and only use it to cook with if it is the only option available at that time. Coconut oil is a saturated fat, but is a medium chain fatty acid which is processed differently in the body than other oils, so I use it regularly. If you choose to eliminate this oil for your own reasons, that is fine, but please note that the flavor of your meal will differ than my intended outcomes. Which brings me to another point. The reason I use raw/unrefined coconut oil, aside from the benefits of lesser processing, is for the flavor it imparts. If you use refined coconut oil, you are getting saturated fats without the health benefits and losing the flavor in the process.

Seeds/Nuts/Grains/Beans: Oats - Oats by nature are gluten free, it is the cross contamination that adds traces of gluten to oats. So if you are celiac or very strict about gluten, oats should be avoided. I am not 100% gluten free, though I lean in that direction, so oats are acceptable in my diet.
Sushi Rice - Sushi rice has a natural stickiness that makes it easy to prepare into beautiful rolls. I love its texture, but it will change the consistency of dishes calling for a basmati or other types of rice. I'm a big fan of using up those leftovers, so feel free to use the sushi rice where you would use regular rice, but with the knowledge that the consistency will be different. Dates - There are many varieties, but the two most common are: Medjool - the plump, sticky, and sugary sweet and Deglet - drier, smaller and less sweet than the Medjool. Both are delicious and bring the nutrition and flavor, but the difference will affect recipes differently. The recipes in this book are based on Medjool dates, so if you are using Deglet, add an extra Deglet for every 2 Medjool called for in the recipe you are preparing, so basically a 3:2 Deglet:Medjool ratio. Sun Dried Tomatoes - They are easily purchased or made. Costco (PriceSmart in Costa Rica) has an excellent option for a good price. If you want to make your own, the recipe is included in the Pantry Prep - Hearty/Earthy section.

Raw Cashews - Technically no cashew can be considered raw as they have to be heated before shelling them to eliminate a toxic compound. However what is deemed a raw cashew, are those that have not received a secondary roasting. If you or a family member have a peanut allergy, cashews can be substituted for peanuts in any of the recipes. Also note that if you have roasted and salted cashews on hand, those can be used in place of the raw, but a salt adjustment will need to be made.

Beans/Legumes: Beans - The magical fruit, are a protein powerhouse and excellent source of fiber. They are also a source of oligosaccharides, which do have health benefits, but their noisy by product when taking your vinyasa, is not so desirable! Soaking beans, helps to leach the oligosaccharides from the legume and reduce the amount of gas experienced a few hours after eating them. The longer you soak them, the less gas. I tend to soak them overnight, but two to three hours is helpful, and will mitigate potential embarrassment. Also, any recipe that calls for black beans, can be substituted with small red beans, not to be confused withthe larger red kidney bean. Canned beans are easy, but I only use them in a pinch to eliminate unnecessary exposure to toxins from the cans and it is better environmentally and financially to buy them in bulk and cook them yourself. Dried beans will last for a long time, but do have a shelf life and should be consumed within a year (less is better) of purchasing them.

Coconut Milk - All recipes that call for coconut milk are based on the coconut milk recipe in this book. If you choose to use canned coconut milk, you will need to dilute the canned milk, which has thickening agents added to them, with one can of water to achieve the correct consistency that is called for in the recipes. Italian Seasoning Blend - You can easily make your own, there is a recipe in the dressing/ condiment section. Or buy a blend already made for ease. For me it all depends on my whereabouts, my kitchen, my garden. I'm on the road and in the air quite a bit, so sometimes the store bought blend is best.

Pantry notes continued...

Miso Paste - This healthy fermented soy bean paste is often attributed to Japanese food, but its origin is actually Chinese. There are several flavors of miso paste and all will work interchangeably with a slightly different flavor outcome. White miso is on the lighter sweeter side, red miso is richer and packs more umami flavor, and yellow miso falls somewhere in the middle of the two. Whichever flavor you choose, do not bring to a boil, in order to preserve its healthful benefits and integrity of its ferments. Miso also makes an excellent marinade (high cooking will lessen the ferments but the flavor is delicious), or is a delicous base for salad dressings.

Tamari/Soy Sauce - Tamari is gluten free soy sauce, and can easily be substituted with regular soy sauce, or Bragg's Liquid Aminos. Bragg's are an excellent option that will slightly affect flavor, but provides essential amino acids for protein synthesis. If you eat only plant based and consume plants from a variety of sources, colors,and textures, you should be getting enough protein, but Bragg's is a tasty way to supplement if you want to be sure.

Cacao Powder - Either raw cacao powder or processed cocoa powder will work in the recipes. I generally strive to use the raw, but if that is not easy to find, or cost prohibitive, there are natural cocoa powders or traditional Dutch process.

Equipment:

Spiralizer - This is a fun gadget and makes noodles out of vegetables in seconds. If you do not have one, simply make noodle ribbons with a vegetable peeler, for an equally beautiful outcome.

Blenders - Any blender will work for these recipes, however the lower powered, old school type will affect the consistency, especially in the mousse, nut mayos, and soups. Even so, there is no need to run out and purchase a 2-3 horsepower blender, unless you really want to get serious about raw nut based desserts, plant based cheeses, and perfect purees.

Glass Jars - Jars are not absolutely necessary, but I find storing the dressings and condiments in glass mason jars, helps keep the fridge organized, while preserving the taste of what is being stored. I use plastic containers when needed, but always opt for glass first or a hard plastic, if available, to eliminate leaching chemicals into the food.

Nut Milk Bag - Yes, the 14 year old in me giggles when I say this... This bag is inexpensive and incredibly helpful when making nut milks and vegan cheeses. You can use a fine mesh strainer if you do not have one, but will not get every last drop from the pulp like you can when squeezing the bag.

Sweeteners:

Honey - I use honey occasionally, but try to limit usage to when I can verify the source. I left honey out of the recipes for various reasons, however if honey is your sweetener of choice, feel free to substitute it for any of the recipes that call for maple syrup or dates. Sugar - I left sugar off the pantry shopping list as it is in only one recipe in the entire book, and even in that recipe, it can be easily substituted. I feel a little sugar in your life is not a big deal, but overdoing it acidifies the body, disrupts a healthy biome, and encourages a host of illnesses. When I refer to sugar, I want to be clear that I am speaking of granulated refined cane sugar. (Naturally occurring sugars do not have the same effects on the body. This is a much debated topic, so I'll leave it at that for now!)

3 Week Guide:

In the following pages, you will find the "3 Week Guide" to help you add more plant based foods into your diet. The guide includes shopping lists for 'Dry Goods' and "Produce', 'Recipe Prep' lists, and 'Full Recipe' lists. Plan your shopping day and a prep day together or on separate days. Perhaps you do your shopping on Saturday, and your prep on Sunday, or in whatever way your week flows. However you choose to do it, it will benefit you to do all the 'Recipe Prep' early in your week. This will facilitate the subsequent speedy preparation of the 'Full Recipes' during your week. Generally if you have all your recipe prep done, each of the Full Meal Recipes shouldn't take more than 30 minutes or so (in prep time, some require longer cooking times) to prepare, making your meals during your busy days easy to handle.

Week 1: Dry Goods

All Oils
All Dried Spices
Salt
Balsalmic Vinegar
Apple Cider Vinegar
Tamari
Chia Seeds
Sushi Nori
Black Sesame Seeds
Dried Coconut
Dates
Tamarind Paste
Sushi Rice
Pad Thai Noodles
Spring Roll Wrappers
Maple Syrup
Peanuts
Dijon Mustard

Week 1: Produce

Mangos
Bananas
Oranges
Apples
Cilantro
Mint
Zucchini
Red Bell Peppers
Carrots
Green Cabbage
Red Cabbage
Beets
Broccoli
Cauliflower
Salad Greens
Cucumbers
Red Onions
Yellow Onions
Garlic
Ginger
Turmeric

Week 1: Recipe Prep

Dijon Vinaigrette
Sesame Vinaigrette
Balsamic Vinaigrette
Peanut Sauce
Quick Pickle Jalapenos
Fried Garlic

Week 1: Full Recipes

Morning Tonic
Date Smoothie
Chia Pudding
Mango Coconut Ice Cream
Baked Bananas
Sushi Bowl
Pad Thai
Asian Style Slaw
Carrot Apple Beet Slaw
Coconut Carrot Soup
Roasted Beet Soup
Spring Rolls

Week 2: Dry Goods

Cashews
Whole Raw Almonds
Sunflower Seeds
Sun Dried Tomatoes
Cacao
Wooden Skewers

Week 2: Produce

Avocados
Bananas
Pineapple
Basil
Cilantro
Tarragon

Red Cabbage
Red Peppers
Crimini Mushrooms
Green Beans
Eggplant
Zucchini

Tomatoes
Cucumber
Carrots
Yellow Onions
Red Onions
Salad Greens
Lettuce

Week 2: Recipe Prep

Sunflower Mayo
Sun Dried Tomatoes in Oil
Sunny Nut Meat
Chocolate Base
Lasagna Tomato Sauce
Roasted Mushrooms
Roasted Red Peppers
Almond Butter

Week 2: Full Recipes

Avocado Mousse
Banana Boats
Lettuce Wraps
Grilled Veggie Skewers
Tarragon Green Beans
Zucchini Noodle Nests
Roasted Tomato Soup
Tacos
Sopa Azteca
Lasagna

Week 3: Dry Goods

Dried Garbanzo Beans
Dried Black Beans
Rice (your favorite type)
Whole Oats
Quinoa
Sliced Almonds
Raisins or Dried Cherries/Cranberries
Tahini
Oregano
Italian Seasoning Blend
Cayenne

Week 3: Produce

Apples
Bananas
Cilantro
Eggplant
Tomatoes
Cucumbers
Red Bell Peppers
Red Onions
Yellow Onions
Yuka
Sweet Potato
Carrot
Celery
Green Plantain
Ripe Plantain
Cooking Greens (kale, chard, spinach...)

Week 3: Recipe Prep

Crisp Topping
Garbanzo Beans
Tico Style Beans
Tahini Sauce
Oat Flour
Hummus
Baba Ghanouj
Falafel Mix

Week 3: Full Recipes

Quinoa Breakfast Bowl
Oatmeal Cookies
Apple Crisp
Roasted Eggplant
Curry Quinoa
Yuka Hash
Greens
Gallo Pinto
Fried Yuka
Gazpacho
Greek Salad Platter
Ron Don

Week 4:

By now you should have purchased all of the dry ingredients and have all the recipe prep completed. You can choose to make any of the Full Recipes that you didn't get to during the previous weeks, or experiment with your own creations. Utilize your stocked pantry and freezer to make your own combinations. This week is a perfect time to make Clean the Fridge Curry, and move out any 'musgo' which is anything that 'must go'!

Pantry Prep: Coconut Milk, Dressings, and Condiments

Coconut Milk

This is a much more simplified process to gathering, husking, cracking and grating your own coconut, and can be applied to most any nut, sunflower seeds, and oats. You can also adjust the ratios to achieve a creamier consistency or one that is more diluted. I prefer a creamy version for coffee or matcha lattes, and cooking in general. Keep in mind that even the creamier version will not be like the 'guar gum' thickened canned milk, but can still be used in place of it. Corn starch is often used to thicken freshly made coconut milk, but I find it unnecessary and rely on the evaporation from slow cooking for more concentrated coconut flavor. All the recipes using coconut milk in this book are based on this recipe. If you use canned coconut milk in lieu of fresh, you will need to add water to balance the consistency. Note that the fats will rise and solidify in the refrigerator, so let it come to room temperature and shake well or gently heat before drinking or adding to beverages.

Makes: 5-6 cups
Prep Time: 10 Minutes
Life Span: 5 days

4 cups Dried Organic Unsweetened Coconut Flakes
8 cups Water

Liquefy in blender for 20-30 seconds and pass through a nut milk bag, squeezing until pulp is dry.

Peanut Sauce

2 1/4 cups Peanuts
2 1/4 cups Coconut Milk
1/2 cup Tahini
1/2 cup Maple Syrup
1/2 T Salt

Blend all ingredients until smooth.

Sesame Vinaigrette

1 1/2 cups Sesame Oil
1/2 cup Apple Cider Vinegar
3/4 cup Tamari
3 inches Chopped Ginger
1/4 cup Maple Syrup
Salt and Pepper
1 tsp Dijon Mustard

Blend well to emulsify.

Balsamic Vinaigrette

1 cup Olive Oil
1/2 cup Balsamic Vinegar
1/4 cup Dijon Mustard
2 T Honey
1/4 medium Red Onion

Blend well to emulsify.

Tahini Sauce

1 1/2 cups Tahini
1 cup Water
1/2 cup Lemon Juice
3 Garlic Cloves
1 tsp Salt (more to taste)

Blend all ingredients until smooth.

Dijon Vinaigrette

Dijon Mustard
Olive Oil
Apple Cider Vinegar

Take a glass jar - any size will do as this recipe is measured in equal proportions. It is a 1:1:1 ratio, so you can measure based on cups or directly into your favorite jar. I use the jar as it is so easy. First, add Dijon mustard to one third of the jar, Second, add the olive oil to bring the jar to about two thirds full, and finally add the Apple Cider Vinegar to finish filling the jar (leaving a bit of headspace at the top for shaking room).
Shake well with each use.

Sunflower Mayo

Makes: about a quart
Prep Time: 15 minutes/4-8 hours soaking time
Storage: One week in the fridge

2 cups Sunflower Seeds - pre-soaked
1 cup Cashews - pre-soaked
1 cup Lemon Juice
4 cloves Garlic
1/2 cup Avocado Oil
2 tsp Salt (more to taste)
Water - just enough to cover the seeds

Drain and rinse the nuts/seeds
Add all ingredients in order
and blend until super creamy.

Tip: If the mixture stops moving before it's perfectly smooth, 'burp' the mixture to release air trapped down by the blade. Turn off the blender (wait for it to stop completely) and insert the blender tamper, or other utensil, to the bottom of the blender pitcher. Resume blending, drizzling water to move the mixture if necessary. Once smooth, let set in refrigerator. It can be used right away, but will thicken up once it is chilled.

Variation: Add a few strips of roasted red pepper for a yummy twist!

Sun Dried Tomatoes in Oil

Makes: 3+ quarts
Prep Time: 45 min - 1 hour
Storage: up to 6 months in the fridge
2 lbs Sun Dried Tomatoes
Pulse the following in a food processor...
4 cups Olive Oil
10 cloves Garlic
1.3 cup Italian Seasoning Blend - dried
2 T Salt

Place the sun dried tomatoes in a large mixing bowl.
Add the herbs, garlic, and olive oil over the tomatoes. Mix well, ensuring that they are all coated in the oil.
Pack the tomatoes in glass jars - to the half way point.
Pour the herbed olive oil until just covering the tomatoes. Pack the rest of the way to the top, and cover with oil.
Leave headspace at the top, about 1/2 inch under the neck.
Pour any remaining herbed oil from the bowl in to the jars, distributing equally between each one.
Add any additional olive oil to make sure they are covered.

Sunny Nut Meat

Makes: 1 1/2 quarts
Prep Time: 15 minutes
Storage: up to 6 months in the fridge

6 cups Sun Dried Tomatoes
6 cups Sunflower Seeds

Place the seeds in the food processor. Pulse to finely chop - be careful not to reduce to a powder, you will want a little texture. Transfer to a mixing bowl. Add the tomatoes and pulse until minced.
Transfer tomatoes to the bowl with the sunflower seeds.
Mix and store in containers.

Italian Seasoning Blend

20 stems fresh Oregano
20 stems fresh Thyme
10 stems fresh Rosemary

Hang herbs to dry (or use your favorite drying method)
Once dry, remove from stem.
Pulse in food processor and store.

Quick Pickle Jalapeños

6-10 Jalepeños
3/4 cup Apple Cider Vinegar

Slice the jalapeños in roughly 1/4 inch coins. Add the jalapeños and vinegar to a small sauce pan. Cover and simmer until jalapeños are soft. Transfer to a container and store for up to a month.

Fried Garlic

1 head Garlic peeled
1/4 cup Avocado Oil

Thin slice the garlic.
Do not preheat the pan.
Add garlic and oil to saute pan.
Heat on low to medium.
Stir continuously until garlic is golden brown. Remove from heat as soon as the color changes.
Transfer to a heat proof container and cool with lid off.
Store in refrigerator for 2 weeks.

Note: Use this for everything to impart a delicious garlicky flavor. Easily double the recipe and make sure to use the oil as well!

Fresco de Tamarindo

A refreshing and delicious drink common in Costa Rica and other Latin American countries.

1 cup Tamarind Sauce
2 quarts water
Mix together and chill
Adjust concentration and sweetness to your palate.

Tamarind Sauce

1 cup Tamarind Paste
(store bought or see note below to make your own)
1 cup Water
6 Dates
Juice of 2 Oranges

Blend all ingredients until pureed.
Heat and Serve.

Note: To make your own paste from the tamarind fruit: Scrape the pulp from 20 pods.
Heat pulp and 1/4 cup of water (add more as needed) to soften, then press through a strainer.

Pantry Prep: Sweet

Almond Butter

Makes: 4 cups
Prep Time: 10 minutes
Storage: 1 month in pantry/3 months in fridge

4 cups Almonds
1 cup Coconut Oil
1/2 cup Maple Syrup
or 1/2 cup Date puree
1 tsp Salt

Blend or process all ingredients until smooth.

Oat Flour

Makes: 8 cups
Prep Time: 10 Minutes
Storage: 1 + month in pantry/ 6 + months in freezer

8 cups Rolled Oats

Blend oats until they resemble flour.
Repeat until finished.
Transfer to a storage container.

Chocolate Base

Makes: about 2 cups
Prep Time: 10 minutes
Storage: 6 months in the fridge

10 Dates
5 T Cacao Powder
1/4 cup Coconut Oil

Combine all ingredients in a food processor.
Pulse to mix then process on high until smooth.

You may need to stop occasionally and scrape the sides with a spatula.

Crisp Topping

Makes: 8 cups
Prep Time: 15 minutes
Storage: 2 weeks in pantry/6 months in freezer

2 cups Oat Flour
2 cups Rolled Oats
2 cups Sugar
2 cups Coconut Oil
1/2 tsp Cinnamon
Pinch of Salt

Note: 1 1/2 cups of Maple Syrup can be subbed for a refined sugar free option, but the mixture must be stored in the fridge or frozen.

Combine all ingredients in a mixing bowl.
Knead with your hands until thoroughly mixed.
Transfer to your crisp and store remaining topping.

Pantry Prep: Hearty/Earthy

Roasted Red Peppers

Prep Time: 30 minutes (varies depending on cooking method)

5 whole Red Bell Peppers

Roast in the oven at 425, on the grill, or place directly on stove burner, turning as needed until mostly charred.
Remove from heat.

Place in a mixing bowl
Cover with a towel to trap the steam.
Leave to cool.
Remove the skin with your hands.
Scrape the seeds with a spoon or knife.
Store in olive oil in a glass jar in the fridge for up to 1 month.

Roasted Mushrooms

Prep Time: 15 minutes active/
40 minutes passive

2 lb Crimini or Portabellas
1/2 cup Balsamic Vinegar
1 cup Tamari
1 cup Olive Oil
light Salt and Pepper

Rinse the mushrooms well and remove any bad or tough stems.
Mix the liquid ingredients.
Marinate the mushrooms - 30 minutes to 24 hours.
Bake for 40 minutes.

Store the liquid to make the Jalẽpeno Balsamic dressing.

Lasagna Tomato Sauce

Makes: 3-4 quarts
Prep Time: 30 minutes active/
1 hour passive

25 Roma Tomatoes
1 head Garlic
5 Red Bell Peppers
20 leaves Basil
1/2 cup Balsamic Vinegar
Salt and Pepper to taste

Chop the ingredients and blend.
Transfer to a stock pot, bring to boil, then reduce to a simmer.
Allow to slow cook and thicken for about an hour.
Pour into containers to cool and then freeze or can.
If using glass jars for freezing, leave an inch of space at the top.

Hummus

Makes: almost 2 quarts
Prep Time: 20 minutes
Storage: Freezes well for up to 6 months

4 cups Cooked Chickpeas
1 cup Tahini
1 cup Lemon Juice
1 T Cumin
4 cloves Garlic
1/4 cup Olive Oil
1 cup Water
Salt and Pepper

Combine all the ingredients and process until creamy.
NOTE: Halve the recipe, and make it in 2 batches if necessary.

Baba Ghanouj

Makes: about 1 1/2 quarts
Prep Time: 20 minutes
Storage: Freezes well for up to 6 months

3 roasted medium Eggplants
1/2 cup Tahini
1/2 cup Lemon Juice
4 cloves Garlic
1 T Cumin
Salt and Pepper

See instructions for Hummus

Falafel Mix

Makes: enough mixture for 20 + falafels
Prep Time: 30 minutes
Storage: Freezes well for up to 6 months

4 cups soaked lentils (soaked for 4-8 hours)
1 small Yellow Onion
1/4 cup Parsley
4 cloves Garlic
1 1/2 T Oat flour
1 1/2 T Salt
1 T Black Pepper
2 tsp Cayenne (more if you like the heat!)
Oil for frying

Set aside the lentils. Pulse all remaining ingredients in the food processor. Add the lentils and pulse until all the ingredients are well blended, but not soft like hummus. More texture will make for a fluffier falafel. Freeze in containers or roll into slightly flattened balls. Pan fry on medium heat for about 3 minutes on both sides.

Tico Style Black Beans (or Red Beans)

Makes: about 2 quarts
Prep Time: 20 minutes active/
2 hours total/4-8 hours soaking
Storage: 5-7 days in fridge/
6+ months in freezer

2 pounds Black Beans (dry weight) soaked
1 whole Habanero Pepper
(optional – will not be overly spicy)
1½ T Salt
Oil for sautéing
1 bunch chopped Cilantro
Dice the following aromatics…
2 medium Yellow Onions
2 stalks Celery
1 Red Bell Pepper

Coat the bottom of a 3 quart stock pot with oil. Add the onions, bell pepper, garlic, and celery. Drain and rinse the soaking beans. Sauté until onions are translucent and begin to caramelize. Add the salt, cilantro, drained beans and habanero, mix well. Add nearly twice as much water as beans. Bring to a boil then reduce heat to a simmer uncovered. Remove the habanero after an hour, if you are sensitive to spicy. Check for sufficient water and add more if beans look dry. Stir the beans occasionally. When they are soft and have thickened, they are ready. Add salt to taste. Transfer to containers, let cool, then freeze.

Garbanzo Beans

Makes: 2 quarts
Prep Time: 5 minutes active/
2 hours total/4-8 hours soaking
Storage: 5-7 days in fridge/
6+ months in freezer

2 pounds Garbanzo Beans
(dry weight) soaked
Place drained and rinsed beans in a 3 quart stock pot. Add double the amount of water. Bring to a boil. Reduce heat, cover, and simmer until soft, about 2 hours.

Garbanzo beans are harder than black or red beans and will cook faster if they have eight hours soak time.

Quinoa

Makes: 6-8 cups
Prep Time: 15 minutes
Storage: 5-7 days in fridge

4 cups dry Quinoa
8 cups water

Make ahead and keep plain Quinoa in the fridge to have ready for the Quinoa Breakfast Bowl, the Curried Quinoa, or a quick lunch or dinner.

Flavor Profile: Sweet

Daily Morning Tonic

1 inch Turmeric Root
1 inch Ginger Root
Squeeze Lemon/Lime
Dash Black Pepper

Grate or chop roots. Combine ingredients. Boil turmeric, ginger, and black pepper together for 5 minutes. Add lemon and serve. Sweeten if you desire.

Date Smoothie

This delicious smoothie masquerades as a milkshake, but with none of the heaviness. Dates are staples in Middle Eastern homes and are part of the Iftar – the meal that breaks the fast in Ramadan. Their ability to satiate hunger and their high nutrient content allows for the observer to break the fast gently. They are loaded with minerals which support strong bones, are high in fiber which aids in digestion, and among many other benefits, can help bump up your love life, so happy dating...

Makes: 2 Large or 4 Small
Prep Time: 10 minutes
Life Span: A few days

2 cups Coconut Milk (or ½ cup Coconut and 2 cups Water)
1 cup Water
2-3 Dates
1 frozen Banana (or 1 Banana and a handful of Ice)
¼ cup Almonds (or ¼ cup Almond Butter)
Small handful of Spinach or your favorite Greens

Blend well and Serve!

Variation: Add ¼ cup of Cacao powder or a tablespoon of Chocolate Base for a decadant treat!

Chia Pudding

The humble chia seed was once a staple crop to Pre-Columbian Meso-Americans. This cousin to mint and tiny powerhouse was used historically by the indigenous Rarámuri(Tarahumara) runners of Mexico to increase stamina, to stave off hunger, and maintain hydration (a concept now known as gel hydration) on runs as long as 200 miles in two days in unforgiving mountainous terrain. It is also an excellent source of omega 3s, protein, iron, calcium, among others, and will provide a lasting satiety due to its gelling action and nutrient profile.

Makes: 8 servings
Prep Time: 15 minutes
Passive Time: 1-8 hours

½ cup Chia seeds
2 cups Coconut milk
1Banana
¼ cup Maple Syrup or 4 Dates
½ tsp Cinnamon
Juice of ½ Lime

Place the chia seeds in a mixing bowl.
Blend together the bananas, coconut milk, cinnamon, maple syrup, and lime juice.
Pour the contents of the blender over the seeds and stir the mixture well.
Cover and place in the fridge overnight.
It can be ready in an hour, but longer allows more gelling and softer consistency.

Variation:
Add ¼ cup cacao powder when blending for added decadence.

Variations are endless!
Pour 2 cups of Date Smoothie Over ½ cup of Chia Seeds and let set overnight.
or
Pick your favorite smoothie and turn it into Chia pudding.

Hot Quinoa Breakfast Bowl

This ancient seed and Incan staple crop is a complete protein, meaning it contains all the essential amino acids necessary for protein synthesis. Its power not only lies in its super high nutrient profile, but in its resiliency as a plant. Spanish colonists made diligent attempts to eradicate quinoa during their efforts to undermine all cultural staples and references of the indigenous Incan. Fortunately, the plant, member of the same family as spinach, Amaranthacea, is a prolific seed producer and it survived to thrive again. Look for quinoa that is fair trade and organic.

Makes: 4 servings
Prep Time: 15 minutes
Storage: 5 days

2 cups cooked Quinoa
2 ripe Bananas
½ cup Sliced Almonds
½ cup Coconut Milk
¼ cup Almond Butter
¼ tsp of Cinnamon (try some cardamom and/or nutmeg if you like)
Pinch of salt
Coconut Oil for sautéing

Heat the quinoa with the coconut milk. Sauté the bananas in coconut oil until golden brown. Watch them, they caramelize fast! Combine everything and fold together. Serve hot for cold mornings or just warmed for summer months.

Variations: Endless! You can add anything that you would normally add to oatmeal.

Variations:
Add a couple of handfuls of blueberries. Try it with stone fruits such as peaches or apricots, or whatever fruit is in season!

Apple Crisp

I honestly cannot remember when I started making this dessert, for nearly 20 years at least. I'm not a baker, my desserts are built the same way that I build savory recipes – to be more forgiving and less reliant on science! The natural flavor, texture, and tartness of the apples perfectly balances the sweet crunchy topping.

Makes: 16 servings
Prep Time: 30 minutes active/45 minutes passive
Storage: 5-7 days in the fridge, can be reheated

10-12 Apples
6-8 cups Crisp Topping
Coconut Oil for greasing

Preheat oven to 375 degrees.
Grease a 4.5 quart (large Pyrex or equivalent size) baking dish with a bit of the coconut oil.
Peel and thinly slice the apples around ¼ inch wide.
Place apples in baking dish up to about ¾ full.
Spread the crisp topping over the apples until evenly and thickly covered.
Bake for 45 minutes to 1 hour (check in 30 minutes to assess) until golden brown and filling is bubbling.

Note: Regarding the topping. You can adjust how much to use after making it a few times. My daughter lays it on thick as she says the topping is the best part!
Note: Regarding the apples. The thickness of the apples is important – too thick and the top will cook faster than the apples, too thin and they become applesauce. The caveat! When substituting soft stone fruit, cutting the fruit thicker is better.

Mango Coconut Ice Cream

Makes: 4 servings
Prep Time: 10 minutes
Storage: 6+ months in freezer

4 cups frozen Mangos
½ cup Coconut Milk
1 T Coconut Oil

Blend all ingredients until smooth.
Serve immediately.
Transfer extra to a container and freeze.

Note:
Keep an extra ½ cup of coconut milk ready and add sparingly if you find the fruit difficult to blend.
When serving ice cream from the freezer – rather than just made, pop it back in the blender for easier serving.

Variations:
Can be made with nearly any fruit. Pineapple is great and Banana is especially delicious on its own or with ¼ to ½ cup Cacao Powder for a rich chocolate treat.

Chocolate Avocado Mousse

Makes: 10 servings
Prep Time: 15 minutes
Storage: 3 days

3 medium ripe Avocados
1¼ cup Coconut Milk
1¼ cup Cacao Powder
½ cup Maple Syrup
2 T Coconut Oil
½ tsp + a pinch Salt

Blend all ingredients until creamy smooth.
Transfer to serving dish(es).
Chill before serving to allow to set.

Note: You can serve immediately, but chilling gives it the mousse-like texture.

Variations: Use water in place of the coconut milk and avocado oil in place of the coconut oil for a more neutral flavor than that of the coconut.

Baked Bananas

6 medium Bananas
¼ cup Maple Syrup
½ cup chopped Cashews
Juice of 1 Orange (or Lime)
Coconut Oil for greasing

Makes: 6 servings
Prep Time: 15 minutes active/45 minutes passive
Storage: 1 week in fridge

Preheat oven to 350.
Grease baking dish.
Peel and cut bananas in half.
Put bananas, maple syrup, and juice in baking dish and mix well.
Sprinkle with sugar. (optional)
Bake 30-45 minutes until caramelized.

Oatmeal Cookies

4 cups Crisp Topping
¼ cup Chia Seeds
1 cup Coconut Milk
¼ cup chopped Cashews
¼ cup chopped Dates

Makes: 15-20
Prep Time: 30 minutes active/12 minutes passive
Storage: 1 week in fridge

Preheat oven to 350.
Soak chia seeds in coconut milk for 15 minutes.
Grease cookie sheet.
Combine all ingredients and mix well.
Spoon slightly flattened balls of dough onto cookie sheet.
Bake for 10-12 minutes.

Ms. LeMaitre's Favorite Banana Boats

Makes: 4 servings
Prep Time: 10 min
Storage: eat immediately

2 Bananas
Almond Butter
Chocolate Sauce
1 Orange
4 Strawberries
Chia Seeds

Slice bananas on the diagonal.
Slice Strawberries
Drizzle with Almond Butter and Chocolate Sauce.
Squeeze fresh OJ over the top.
Sprinkle with Chia Seeds.

Variation:
Serve with Pineapple Coconut Ice Cream
for a healthy twist on a banana split.

Flavor Profile: Light/Bright

Asian Inspired Slaw

Makes: 8 servings
Prep Time: 30 minutes
Storage: 5 days

Julienne the following...
2 medium Carrots
1 Red Bell Pepper
1 small Red Onion
½ Green Cabbage
¼ Red Cabbage
Cut into small florets...
½ whole Broccoli
½ whole Cauliflower

Chop...
½ cup Peanuts
8 Mint leaves
4 stems Cilantro
Toss all veggies together with...
1+ cup Sesame Vinaigrette

Let marinate for 15 minutes before serving.
Serve over a bed of greens or as is...

Pico de Gallo

A small bit of confusion ensued when I was once asked to make Chimichurri and I produced a delicious garlicky green sauce rooted in Argentinian cuisine. I later learned that in Costa Rica, Pico de Gallo is commonly known as Chimichurri…

3 Tomatoes cubed
1 small Red Onion diced
1 bunch Cilantro chopped
Juice of 1 Lime
Salt to taste

Note: If you do not have a love affair with cilantro like I do, then cut down the quantity to suit your palate.

Tip: If you are sensitive to raw onions, soak your onions in the lime juice while chopping the other ingredients. The acids in the lime juice subdue the intensity of the onions.

Cabbage Salad

This is a staple served on the side of nearly every dish in Costa Rica. The bright hits of lime and the crunchy texture pair well with their hearty rice and bean dishes.

½ Green Cabbage
1 small Carrot (optional)
1 bunch Cilantro
Juice of 2 Limes
Salt to taste

Julienne the veggies.
Chop the cilantro.
Toss with lime juice.

Variations:
Add shredded carrots and red cabbage for variety.

Carrot Apple Beet Slaw

Grate the following...
2 small Beets
2 medium Carrots
1 large Apple
2 inches peeled Ginger
Toss together with...
Juice of 2 Oranges
1 T Maple Syrup
Salt to taste

Let marinate for 15 minutes

Quick Pickle Cucumber Ribbons

1 Cucumber
¾ cup Apple Cider Vinegar
1 T Agave

Using a vegetable peeler
Peel the first layer of skin in one motion.
Using the same motion, "peel" ribbons of the cucumber until you reach the seeded center.
Turn the cucumber and repeat, until only the center remains.
Combine all ingredients
Let marinate for 15 minutes

Tip: Any left over Carrot,
Beet Slaw can be used in this recipe.

Roasted Beet Soup

Makes: 10 servings
Prep Time: 20 minutes active/1½ hours passive
Storage: 5 days

4 medium Beets
1 large Yellow Onion
¼ cup Olive oil
4 cups Orange juice
2 cups Water
Salt and Pepper

Preheat oven to 350.
Peel and cut beets and onion into large chunks.
Mix veggies together on a baking sheet.
Coat veggies in the olive oil.
Season with salt and pepper.
Cover and roast for one hour.
Remove cover and roast for ½ hour more or until beets are fork tender.
Transfer to blender.
Add orange juice and water and blend until velvety smooth.

Tips:
This soup freezes well or perhaps there is a neighbor that needs a meal. This can be served warm or hot so is great year round. This recipe is easily halved for half the active prep time.
If your finished soup is not like velvet, add some extra coconut milk while blending.
Delicious served with Carrot Apple Beet Slaw.

Coconut Carrot Soup

Makes: 15 servings
Prep Time: 30 minutes active/45 minutes passive
Storage: 5 days in fridge/6+ months in freezer

10 medium Carrots
4 medium Yellow Onions
1 Jalapeño (optional but delicious)
6 cloves Garlic
1 quart Coconut Milk
1 cup of Coconut Oil
Salt and Pepper to taste

Preheat oven to 350.
Peel and cut carrots and onions into large chunks
Spread all veggies onto 2 baking sheets.
Season with salt and pepper.
Add coconut oil.
Mix everything together ensuring all veggies are coated in oil – use your hands, coconut oil is good for them!
Roast in oven for 30-45 minutes.
Watch for the veggies to caramelize. When carrots are fork tender, they are done.
Transfer to blender – this will take 2 batches. Make sure to scrape all the flavor bits from the baking tray.
Blend the roasted veggies with the coconut milk until velvety smooth. Remember 2 batches.
Transfer to a pot on the stove to simmer or to containers to freeze, or both.

Tip: I keep the broth and the diced veggies separate until ready to serve, as the veggies can be used as salad toppings, and the broth as salad dressing.

Gazpacho

Makes: 8 servings
Prep Time: 30 minutes
Storage: 3-5 days

Large chop and combine the following in the blender…
4 Tomatoes
1 Bell Pepper
¼ Red Onion
1 T Balsamic Vinegar
½ cup Olive Oil
8 leaves Basil
2 cloves Garlic
Salt and Pepper
Dice the following and toss together…
1 Tomato or a few cherry tomatoes
½ Red Bell Pepper
½ Red Onion
1 large Cucumber

Sushi Bowl

This dish was inspired by the desire to have a sushi roll, but lacking the time and staff (and energy!) to make 100+ of them for the guests. This recipe reconfigures all the elements of my vegan sushi vision in to an easy to make quick bowl.

Makes: 8 servings
Prep Time: 30 minutes
Storage: 3 days

2 cups Sushi Rice (dry measure)
Julienne the following ingredients...
1 large Carrot
½ large Cucumber
½ Red Bell Pepper
Cube the following ingredients...
½ Mango
1 Avocado
With scissors, cut into strips...
½ sheet Sushi Nori or 4 sheets Roasted Sushi Snacks
Finish with...
Black Sesame Seeds
Sesame Vinaigrette

Cook the Sushi Rice, once finished, transfer to a baking sheet or large mixing bowl to cool until lukewarm. Add all ingredients to cooled rice, except the Avocado and Sushi Nori strips. Mix well and then add the Avocado and Sushi Nori, gently mixing until distributed evenly.

Variation:
Mango Sticky Rice
Combine 4 cups Coconut Milk with ½ cup Maple Syrup and ½ tsp Salt. Use this mixture in place of water to cook your rice.
Transfer to plates.
Top with chunks of Mangos.
Sprinkle with Black Sesame Seeds.

Lettuce Wraps

One of my favorites, and fast! The nutrient dense mushrooms and cashews satiate without heaviness. The Quick Pickle Cucumbers give the earthy mushrooms a nice brightness and the Sesame Vinaigrette rounds out the dish. This dish stands on its own as it is, or the filling can be served over rice or on a bed of greens for variety.

Makes: 4-6 servings
Prep Time: 30 minutes
Storage: 5 days

2 large Carrots
2 cups Roasted Mushrooms
2 cups Cashews (Peanuts substitute well)
½ Red Onion
2 cloves Garlic
10-12 leaves Basil
Sesame Oil for light sautéing
Sesame Vinaigrette
Quick Pickle Cucumbers

Combine onions, garlic, and basil in the bowl of the food processor.
Pulse until minced.
Add to large oiled pan, sauté on low so as to maintain the texture of the mixture.
Repeat with mushrooms, then carrots, then cashews.
Transfer to a large mixing bowl.
Season with Salt and Pepper to taste.
Top with Sesame Vinaigrette and Quick Pickle Cucumber strips.

Variations:
Use peanuts in place of cashews.
Also delicious with Peanut Sauce.

Note: If you don't have roasted mushrooms already prepared, substitute 2 medium Portabellas or 8 large Criminis and 1 tablespoon Tamari, and follow the same instructions.

Spring Rolls

Makes: One rice paper makes 1
Prep Time: 30-45 minutes
Storage: 2 days

Pack of Spring Roll Wrappers
¼ Pack of Rice Noodles
Peanut Sauce
Julienne any veggie or combination of...
Cucumbers
Carrots
Beets
Zucchini
Bell Peppers
Chop...
Mint
Cilantro

Heat (comfortable to touch) a half inch of water in a sauté pan that is equal to or larger than the rice paper.
Place one rice paper in the pan until softened then lay it on a flat surface.
Add a few strands of noodles and about a ½ cup of veggies to the center of the rice paper, but slightly closer to you. Lift the curve closest to you, pinched between both index fingers and thumbs.
With the remaining fingers, pull the ingredients close to the lifted paper and begin to roll.
Fold the side flaps, one at a time and continue to roll until closed and tight.
Serve with Peanut Sauce.

Tip:
This is an excellent way to use left over
Asian Inspired Slaw, Pad Thai,
Carrot Apple Beet Slaw
or any veggies that need to
be used. It takes practice, so don't
get discouraged!

Tip: The curry powder can be adjusted as it is super strong in this recipe. I like the intensity of it with the slightly bitter flavor, and the added turmeric is a healthy bonus.

Make your own Curry Powder:

3 tsp ground turmeric
1 tsp ground cumin
1 tsp ground mustard seed
1 tsp ground coriander
1 tsp ground cardamom
1 tsp ground cinnamon

Variations:

Serve hot, topped with Roasted Eggplant and a drizzle of Tahini Sauce.
Or at room temperature on greens or as as a lettuce wrap.

Curried Quinoa

Makes: 4 servings
Prep Time: 30 minutes
Storage: 5-7 days

Combine in a mixing bowl...
2 cups cooked Quinoa
¼ diced Red Onions
¼ cup dried Raisins
¼ cup chopped Cashews
1 T chopped Cilantro
1 T chopped Mint
Then add...
½ cup Curry Powder
¼ cup Apple Cider Vinegar
3 T Avocado Oil
¼ cup Maple Syrup
2 inches grated Ginger
Salt and pepper to taste

Mix well
Transfer to plates
Garnish with
Quick Pickle Cucumber

Pad Thai

This colorful dish is a loose interpretation of a traditional Pad Thai anchored by a few key flavors - the tamarind sauce, the fried garlic, and the marinated jalapeños.

Julienne the following veggies...
2 medium Carrots
½ Green or Napa Cabbage
¼ Red Cabbage
½ Red Bell Pepper
½ Red Onion
Bunch of Dark Leafy Greens
Cut...
1 small Zucchini in half moons
1 head of Broccoli in florets

Pre-heat oven to 350.
Spread Broccoli on baking sheet and drizzle enough coconut oil to cover each piece, and season with salt and pepper.
Roast for about 25 minutes.
Add a drizzle of coconut oil to a warmed sauté pan and sauté each type of vegetable separately, lightly salting as you go. Sauté the veggies for just a couple of minutes to retain color, texture, flavor, and nutrients. Use a baking sheet to place the cooked vegetables on for them to cool.
Turn off the oven and pull out the broccoli, coat in the tamarind sauce and replace in the oven to stay warm while you finish up.
Toss all veggies together when cool. When you are ready to serve, reheat just enough to warm, but maintain color and texture. Serve immediately over Rice Noodles and topped with the Tamarind Glazed Broccoli.
Finish with the Peanut Sauce.
Garnish with the Fried Garlic and Pickled Jalapeños!

Flavor Profile: Hearty/Earthy

Tarragon Green Beans

Makes: 4 servings
Prep Time: 20 minutes
Storage: 5 days

1 lb Green Beans stems removed
16 Cherry Tomatoes halved
½ Red Onion shaved
1 T chopped Tarragon
Dijon Vinaigrette
Salt and Pepper to taste

Variation:
Haricot verts, French for green bean, are a slimmer style of green beans, that are a super tender and delicious alternative in this recipe.

Note:
2 diced Roma tomatoes can be substituted for the cherry tomatoes.

Blanche green beans.
Toss all veggies together.
Drizzle with Dijon Vinaigrette.
Serve chilled as a salad or warmed as a side dish.

Zucchini Noodle Nests

Makes: 4+ servings
Prep Time: 20 minutes
Storage: 3-5 days

1 medium Zucchini
½ cup Sunny Nut Meat
8 leaves chopped fresh Basil
¼ cup Sliced Almonds
1 tsp Salt (+ more to taste)

Spiralize zucchini,
Place in a mixing bowl,
Add salt and let rest for 15 minutes.
Transfer to a colander and let drain.
Mix in remaining ingredients

Variation: Lightly steam or sauté the zucchini for a different texture.

Note: If you don't have a spiralizer, you can make ribbons by using a vegetable peeler.
Shave the zucchini on the same side until reaching the middle, turn, repeat.

Roasted Tomato Soup

Makes: 10-12 Servings
Prep Time: 15 minute active/45 passive
Storage: In the fridge for 5 days

6 medium Tomatoes
1 large Yellow Onion
5 cloves Garlic
Avocado Oil
Salt and Pepper to taste

Preheat oven to 350.
Quarter tomatoes and onions.
Spread on a baking sheet
Drizzle olive oil and mix until everything is well coated in oil.
Roast in oven for 30-45 minutes or until the the edges of the tomatoes begin to char.
Remove from oven and transfer to blender. Add water until the soup has a creamy consistency.

Miso Soup

Makes: 2 quarts – easily halved
Prep Time: 30 minutes
Storage: 5-7 days

1 lb Mushrooms
2 medium Yellow Onions, julienned
5 cloves minced Garlic
2 inches grated Ginger
2 ½ quarts Water
1 cup Miso
½ cup Tamari
1 Sushi Nori sheet cut into strips
Avocado Oil for sautéing

In a medium saucepan, sauté the onions until translucent. Add the mushrooms, garlic, ginger, and sauté until onions and mushrooms are caramelized. Add tamari, water and miso and mix well. Slowly heat on medium. If it starts to boil, lower the heat. Can be ready super quick. Once the soup is hot and the miso is dissolved, it is ready. It will continue to get more flavorful if you let it continue to simmer, on low, for an extra half hour. Top with sushi nori strips and serve.

Variation: Add an inch of grated turmeric and a few handfuls of greens. I love adding Nettles to this dish in spring for added medicinal benefits and deliciousness! Or some coconut milk and quinoa...

Tip: Substitute fresh Mushrooms for already prepared Roasted Mushrooms. To do so, cut the tamari measurement in half for the soup.

Note: Miso is super nourishing and a fermented food. Fermented foods are an important piece in maintaining a healthy gut biome. A healthy gut is directly linked to better mental health.

Ron Don

Makes: 4 quarts, easily halved (or quartered)
Prep Time: 1 hour
Storage: 5 days, freezes well

Dice the following aromatics...
4 Red Bell Peppers
4 Yellow Onions
2 stems Celery
1 bunch Cilantro
1 head Garlic minced
2 inches Turmeric
Cube the following...
4 green Plantains
4 large Sweet Potatoes
2 small Yukas
2 medium Carrots
3 Liters Coconut Milk
1 Liter Water

Sauté the aromatics until they are caramelized,
Add the vegetables, mix well, to coat the
veggies and distribute the aromatics.
Add coconut milk and simmer without lid.
When the soup boils down, add the water
and continue to boil (slow) until the vegetables are soft.
Add more water if it is too thick or when reheating.

Black Bean Puree

Makes: 1 quart
Prep Time: 10 minutes
Storage: 5-7 days in fridge/
6+ months in freezer

1 quart Tico Style Beans
¾ cup Pico de Gallo and
liquid (optional)
3 cups Water

Add Pico de Gallo and beans to the blender. Add just enough water to cover the beans.
Blend until pureed.
If the beans are not pureeing easily, drizzle water slowly into the pitcher to help move the beans.
You may need to stop and scrape the sides of the blender, then continue blending until smooth.

Serve with Patacones and RonDon

Patacones

Makes: about 15
Prep Time: 25 minutes
Storage: best eaten immediately

3 green Plantains
Salt
Avocado Oil for frying
Small plate

Peel the plantains. Cut in 1 ½ to 2 inch pieces.
Fill a medium to large sauté pan 1/3 of the way full with avocado oil and heat to medium-high. Place all the pieces in the hot oil, turning until all sides are bright golden yellow.
Set up your smashing station with a smooth surface and the plate. Remove the pieces from oil and when cool enough to touch, place on the smooth surface and smash to about ½ inch thick with the plate.
Return to the oil and continue frying until crispy.
Salt and Serve...

Tacos

Makes: 4 servings
Prep Time: 45 minutes
Storage: 3-5 days

12 leaves Red Cabbage
Veggie Filling
Sunny Nut Meat
Pico de Gallo
Cabbage Slaw
Sunflower Mayo
Avocado
Cilantro

Variation: Make them like street tacos in warmed corn tortillas filled with Sunny Nut Meat, Cabbage Slaw, and Pico de Gallo, and use the Veggie Filling as a side dish.

Serve with Tico Style Beans and Rice

Sopa Azteca

Costa Rican style tortilla soup

Makes: 15/easily halved
Prep Time: 15 minutes prep/30 minutes passive
Storage: 5-7 days in fridge/6+months in freezer.

12 Tomatoes cubed
1 Yellow Onion diced
6 cloves Garlic minced
1 quart Veggie Filling
1 bunch Cilantro
Handful Corn Chips
Avocado Oil for Sautéing
1 T Salt

Tip: Throw any extra veggies or Pico de Gallo in with this to simmer. Delicious with sweet potato and/or winter squash.

In a stock pot, sauté the onions until caramelized.
Add the cilantro, tomatoes and water.
Simmer the mixture for 15 minutes.
Add the veggie filling and continue to simmer for 15-20 minutes longer. Adjust seasoning, the main seasoning is in the veggie filling. Add the following to taste; cumin, chili powder, salt, and pepper.

Serve with avocado, and Pico de Gallo.
Also delicious with a drizzle of Sunflower Mayo.

Veggie Filling

Makes: 15 easily halved
Prep Time: 30 Minutes
Storage: 5-7 days in fridge

Thick Julienne the following…
4 medium Onions
3 medium Carrots
2 Red Bell Peppers
1 small Zucchini
Mince the following…
1 Jalapeño (optional)
10 cloves Garlic
----
2 cob Corn kernelled
2 T Cumin
2 T Chili Powder
½ tsp Cinnamon
Salt and Pepper

Tip: Use any leftovers for Sopa Azteca or serve with quinoa, rice and beans, baba ghanouj…

Sauté the onions and peppers for about 5 minutes.
Add the spices and garlic and continue sautéing until the onions are caramelized.
Add the rest of the veggies, sauté on high until veggies are al dente.

Gallo Pinto

This is a traditional breakfast (but is great for any meal) in Costa Rica, and is generally served with eggs, meat, and cheese. This is the plant based version, but enjoy in whatever way suits you!

Makes: 4 servings
Prep Time: 30 minutes (if using leftover rice)
Storage: 5 days

Small dice the following aromatics…
½ Red Bell Pepper
½ Yellow Onion
½ stalk Celery
4 cloves Garlic
Mix together…
1 cups Tico Style Beans
1 cups cooked Rice (use leftover rice)

Sauté the aromatics until gently caramelized.
Add the rice and beans.
Heat thoroughly.
Serve with Sweet Plantains, Cabbage Salad, and
Quick Pickle Jalapeños (if you like the heat!).

Sweet Plantains

Sweet Plantains or 'maduros', in Costa Rica, are incredibly versatile and are often used in savory dishes such as the thick coconut stew, Ron Don. They are starchier than bananas, but like bananas the sweetness is dependent on its degree of ripeness. However they will still hold up well to cooking heat, even in their ripest form when the skin is nearly black. The cooking method depends on your dietary needs. I love slicing them and pan frying them in coconut oil. But I wouldn't recommend that daily. For healthier options, they can be boiled without oil, or baked, with a light coating of oil. Any way you decide to prepare them, they are a delicious and healthy addition to Gallo Pinto and many other dishes, as well as a nice treat for dessert.

Variations to the Greek Salad:
Mix with some quinoa and fresh parsley as a take on the classic Tabouli.

Single Serving 'Tabouli':

½ cup Quinoa plain
½ cup Greek Salad
1 T fresh Parsley minced

Greek Style Salad and Mediterranean Inspired Platter

Makes: 10
Prep Time: 15 minutes
Storage: 3-5 days

5 medium Tomatoes cubed
2 large Cucumbers cubed
2 cups Chickpeas cooked
1 Red Bell Pepper diced
1 large Red Onion diced
1 T Pickled Jalapeños
1 T Oregano
½ cup Apple Cider Vinegar
Salt and pepper to taste

Combine all ingredients in a bowl. Let rest for a few minutes, mixing intermittently to disperse the vinegar. Serve on bed of your favorite salad greens with Hummus, Baba Ghanouj, Falafel, Roasted Eggplant and top with Tahini Sauce, or Dijon Vinagrette.

Roasted Eggplant

3 medium Eggplants
Avocado Oil
Salt and Pepper

Slice eggplants about ¾ inch thick.
Lay out in one layer on baking tray.
Brush both sides generously with Oil
Salt and Pepper both sides as well.
Roast for 30 minutes.

Top with roasted red pepper Sunflower Mayo or Tahini Sauce.
Serve alone or with Greek Salad, Curry Quinoa, Zucchini Noodle Nests, Rice...

Tip:
Save leftovers for Baba Ghanouj...

Tip: Yuka is very absorbent of the oil. To achieve the golden brown crispy bottom, you may need to experiment with the amount of oil you use as it is also affected by the type of cookware you use. Also, if you eat eggs, add them on top once the yuka is just about done, then finish in the oven.

Yuka Hash

Makes: 6-8 servings
Prep Time: 30 minutes
Storage: 3-5 days

Cube the following...
1 large Yuka
1 white Sweet Potato
Dice the following...
1 medium Yellow Onion
½ Red Bell Pepper
10 cloves Garlic
Salt and pepper
Avocado Oil for Sautéing

Boil yuka and sweet potato until soft, drain, and set aside. In a large sauté pan, sauté onion, pepper, and garlic. Stir in the yuka and sweet potato and raise the heat. Mix well and let cook until the mixture begins to brown. Move the mixture one more time then spread evenly, covering the bottom of the pan and touching the sides. Let cook until the bottom is golden brown and crispy.

Serve with Greens and Tomato Sauce.

Save any leftovers for Ron Don.

Greens

Makes: 6-8 servings
Prep Time: 30 min
Storage: 5 days

2 lbs Greens
2 small Yellow Onions
12 cloves Garlic
¼ cup Tamari
Splash Balsamic
Salt and Pepper

Cut the greens in large pieces – about 2"x2"
Sauté the garlic and onions until caramelized.
Add the greens and tamari.
Sauté until tender.

Note: Different greens will cook at different paces. To mix them, cut the heartier greens, like kale, in smaller pieces to cook faster.

Make it in two batches or two skillets. Or halve the recipe for a smaller amount.

Make Extra: These greens are so versatile. Use them in Pad Thai or Miso Soup. Serve them with the Greek Platter, Yuka Hash, Roasted Eggplant...

Yuka Fries

Makes: 4 servings
Prep Time: 20 active/ 15 passive
Storage:

1 large Yuka
Oil for Frying
Salt

Peel and cut yuka into large batons.
Boil until fork tender.
Drain and set aside.
Add oil to a sauté pan, about a ¼ way up the pan.
Heat to medium-high.
Test with a small piece to see if the oil is ready.
If it bubbles around it, then it is ready.
Lay the yuka in the pan with space between each one.
Fry on both sides, about 3 or 4 minutes each side.
They are ready when crispy and golden.

Serve with Tomato Sauce.

Tip: Cube any
leftovers and add
them to RonDon.

Tip: Leftovers are great the next day or throw them in when making Baba Ghanouj.
No grill no problem:
Spread the veggies on a baking tray.
Add oil, salt, and pepper.
Roast on 425 until done.

Grilled Vegetable Skewers

Makes: 8 servings (about 25 skewers)
Prep Time: 45 minutes
Storage: 5 days

Cut the following in large chunks...
3 Eggplant
3 Zucchini
3 Red Bell Pepper
3 Red Onions
1 lb Mushrooms (more if you like)
1 Pineapple
Avocado Oil

Skewer the vegetables in any pattern. Fire up the grill on high for 5-10 minutes, reduce to low to medium heat. Lay them out in a pan and brush generously with oil on both sides.
Season with salt and pepper.
Place on the grill and close lid, check them in about 7 minutes. Turn the skewers when the vegetables are well marked from the grill. Remove when both sides are marked.

Serve with
Tarragon Green Bean Salad, rice, and Jalapeño Balsamic Vinaigrette. Also delicious with plain or Curry Quinoa.

Lasagna

Makes: 10-12 servings
Prep Time: 45 minutes prep/
1 hour 15 min cooking
Storage: 5 days

Tip: I love this Lasagna served with a simple salad dressed in Balsamic Vinaigrette. The light and cool crisp salad balances the hearty tomato sauce. Leftovers are delicious served over rice or quinoa.

6 cups Tomato Sauce
4 cups Sunny Nut Meat
3 cups Roasted Mushrooms
2 Roasted Red Peppers
Slice the following into long strips, like lasagna noodles...
3 Eggplants
3 Zucchinis

Preheat the oven to 350.
In a large Pyrex, layer the ingredients in this order:

- Zucchini
- Eggplant
- Mushrooms
- Sweet pepper
- Tomato Sauce
- Sun Dried Tomato Filling

Repeat until about ½ inch from the top of the Pyrex.
Cover the top layer well with sauce and top with Sunny Nut Meat.
Cover with foil and bake for 1 hour. After 1 hour, remove the foil and continue cooking for 15-20 more minutes. Remove from oven, and carefully tilt to drain any excess liquid.
Let rest for 10 minutes, cut and serve.

Clean the Fridge Curry

Makes: 15 servings
Prep Time: 30 minutes active/
30 minutes passive
Storage: 5-7 days

Tip: As the name implies, go through your fridge and pull out leftovers and add in somewhat equal proportions to the ingredients listed in the recipe. The items in parentheses are suggested leftovers to use. Don't be afraid to experiment, this soup is very forgiving!

4 Tomatoes (pico de gallo, greek salad, tomato sauce)
3 Carrots (carrot soup)
2 Sweet Potatoes
2 Yellow Onions
2 Red Bell Peppers (roasted red peppers)
½ Yuka (yuka hash, yuka fries)
1 head Garlic
1 medium Zucchini (veggie skewers, roasted eggplant and/or mushrooms)
1 quart Coconut Milk
½ cup Curry Powder
2 T Cumin
2 tsp Cinnamon
3 T Salt

Sauté onions, garlic, and red bell pepper until they are caramelized.
Add the curry, cinnamon and salt to bloom the spices. Add the remaining vegetables, mix well, and let cook for about 5 minutes. Add the coconut milk and bring to simmer. Cook with the lid on low heat for 30 minutes, then remove the lid and cook for 20 more minutes to thicken.

Photo Credit: Jeff Cochran

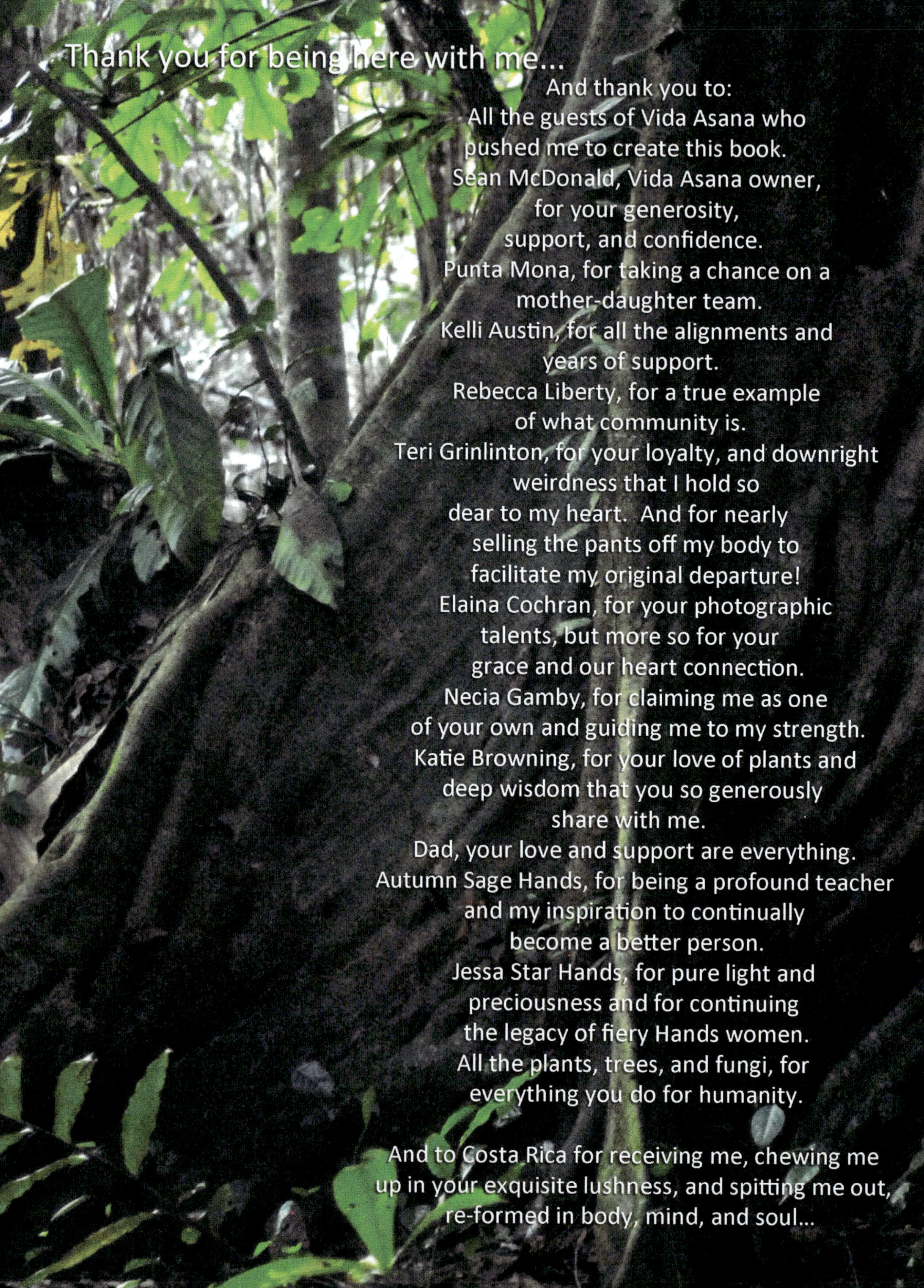

Thank you for being here with me...

And thank you to:
All the guests of Vida Asana who
pushed me to create this book.
Sean McDonald, Vida Asana owner,
for your generosity,
support, and confidence.
Punta Mona, for taking a chance on a
mother-daughter team.
Kelli Austin, for all the alignments and
years of support.
Rebecca Liberty, for a true example
of what community is.
Teri Grinlinton, for your loyalty, and downright
weirdness that I hold so
dear to my heart. And for nearly
selling the pants off my body to
facilitate my original departure!
Elaina Cochran, for your photographic
talents, but more so for your
grace and our heart connection.
Necia Gamby, for claiming me as one
of your own and guiding me to my strength.
Katie Browning, for your love of plants and
deep wisdom that you so generously
share with me.
Dad, your love and support are everything.
Autumn Sage Hands, for being a profound teacher
and my inspiration to continually
become a better person.
Jessa Star Hands, for pure light and
preciousness and for continuing
the legacy of fiery Hands women.
All the plants, trees, and fungi, for
everything you do for humanity.

And to Costa Rica for receiving me, chewing me
up in your exquisite lushness, and spitting me out,
re-formed in body, mind, and soul...

Photo Credit: Jeff Cochran

A little about the Author...

Plant obsessed and adventure ready, Heather Hands explores the world through the lens of food, nature, and culture. The observations that arise from her travels are used to further her work of 20+ years in seeking to understand and define community, from multiple perspectives, and how it fits in the post-modern, technology driven world. Her work with food encompasses the entire cycle from seed to seed and has been a pursuit for much of her life. Heather's next project takes her on the road, through the US and abroad, to further engage with the community at large and explore innovations and solutions to the complexities of building true inclusive community.